LIFE AND DEATH IN A

HILL FORT

Written by
Juliet Kerrigan

Illustrated by
Martin Bustamante

Collins

Welcome to the Iron Age

Britain 2,000 years ago was a land of hills, forests
and wide rivers. This was the Iron Age, when people
lived in large family groups on small farms. They grew
wheat and barley and had animals like cows, sheep
and chickens. Oxen pulled simple ploughs to prepare
the fields for sowing crops.

Everyone drank beer and ate vegetable soups and stew, bread and porridge. Meat was only for special occasions. Food was cooked over an open fire in iron cauldrons or clay pots.

People lived in round houses, probably with thatched roofs.

The walls were made of a mix of straw and mud, called "daub".

No one could read or write, but Iron Age people knew how to spin and weave wool to make clothes. We don't know exactly what their clothes looked like, because only tiny pieces of fabric have survived.

There were no shops. Animals, wool or iron could be bartered, sometimes using special tokens made of tin and bronze called "potin coins".

Salt was also bartered. It was very valuable to Iron Age people because it was used to preserve meat. It was also rubbed into animal skins before they were turned into leather.

This woman is weaving cloth on a loom.

Iron Age coin showing a horse

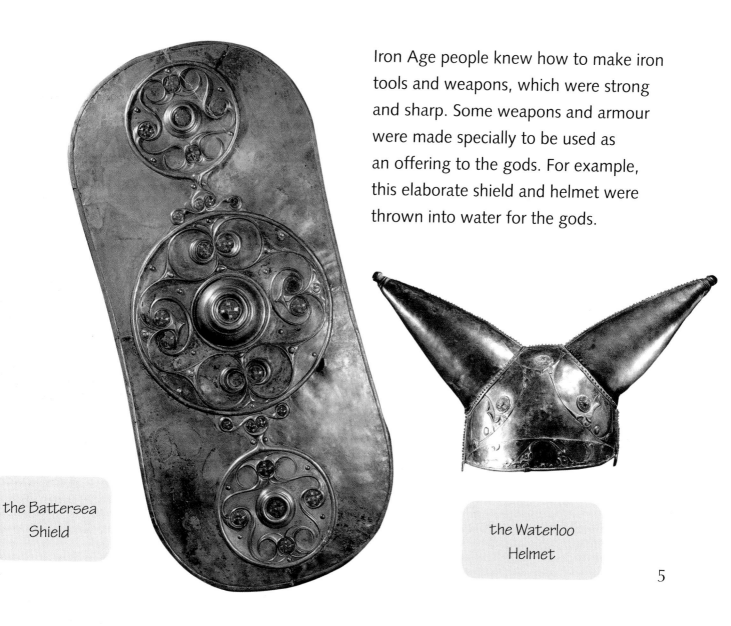

Iron Age people knew how to make iron tools and weapons, which were strong and sharp. Some weapons and armour were made specially to be used as an offering to the gods. For example, this elaborate shield and helmet were thrown into water for the gods.

the Battersea Shield

the Waterloo Helmet

5

Building on a hill

Life wasn't always peaceful in the Iron Age. Weapons were used for battle, not just as offerings to the gods. Different groups may have fought each other to protect their families, animals and land.

To defend themselves, Iron Age people built large structures on top of hills, which we call hill forts. They may have lived on their farms, but would have rushed to the hill fort when they were in danger.

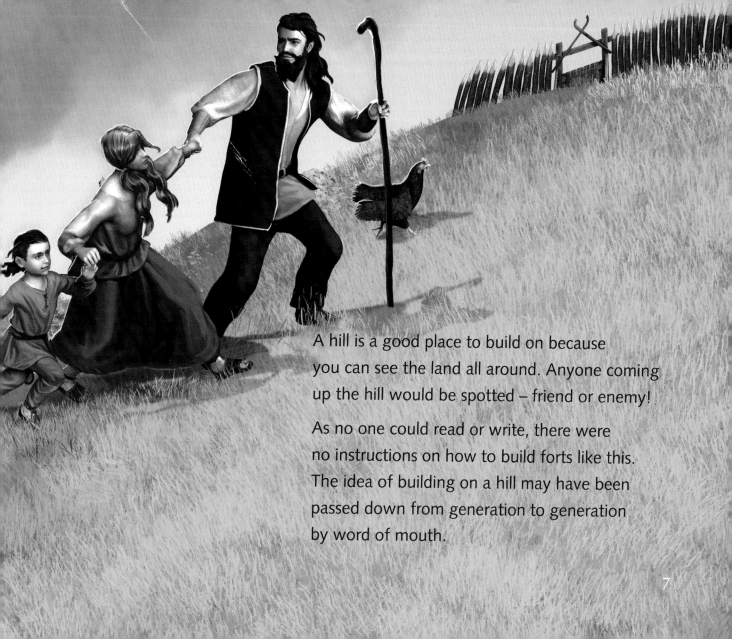

A hill is a good place to build on because you can see the land all around. Anyone coming up the hill would be spotted – friend or enemy!

As no one could read or write, there were no instructions on how to build forts like this. The idea of building on a hill may have been passed down from generation to generation by word of mouth.

Most hill forts were built in a similar way. This suggests that building methods were passed between family groups or by people travelling from one part of the country to another.

To make a hill fort, a wall of earth, called a rampart, is built around the top of the hill. Some ramparts were 10 metres high above the ditch.

The size of the fort depended on the size of the hill, but it would have taken lots of people to build it, possibly hundreds. Men, women and children would have worked on the fort, as well as farming their own land. A leader or chief may have been in charge of the building work.

Hill Fort Fact

Hill forts built on land where there is a lot of chalk would have looked bright white when new.

Iron Age people used tools made from deer antlers and ox shoulder blades to dig out the earth. Antlers and ox bones were found in an Iron Age hill fort.

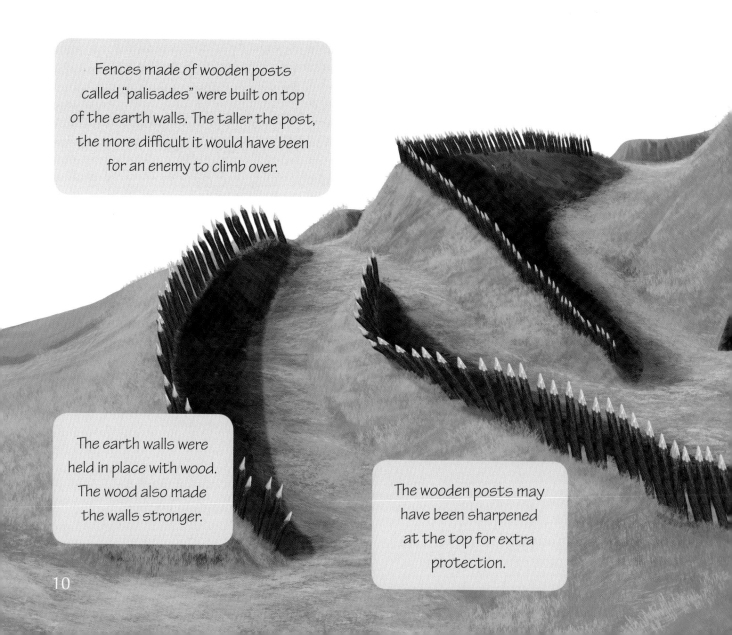

Fences made of wooden posts called "palisades" were built on top of the earth walls. The taller the post, the more difficult it would have been for an enemy to climb over.

The earth walls were held in place with wood. The wood also made the walls stronger.

The wooden posts may have been sharpened at the top for extra protection.

10

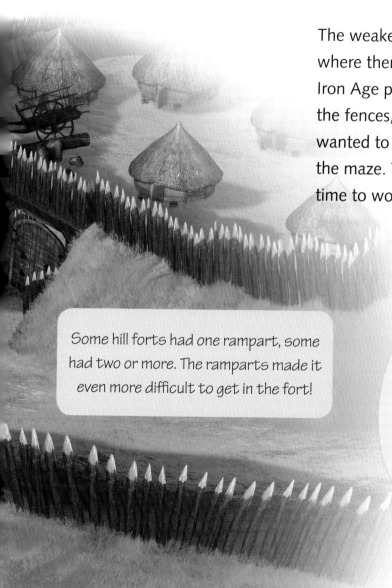

The weakest parts of a hill fort were the entrances, where there were gates. To protect the gateways, Iron Age people built up mounds of earth outside the fences, to create a maze-like path. If anyone wanted to get in the gates, they had to follow the maze. This gave the people inside the fort time to work out if they wanted to let them in.

Some hill forts had one rampart, some had two or more. The ramparts made it even more difficult to get in the fort!

Hill Fort Fact

The gateway often faced east, towards the rising sun. This meant it would be the first part of the fort to have light in the morning.

Buried bones

Archaeologists have found evidence, such as skeletons, that show there was fighting at some of the hill forts. In one skeleton, the weapon that probably killed the victim was still embedded in his spine. Injuries made by iron spears, javelins and swords were found on other skeletons.

About 11,000 smooth pebbles, called sling stones, were found in another hill fort. Warriors would have put them in slings made of animal skin and fired them at the enemy below.

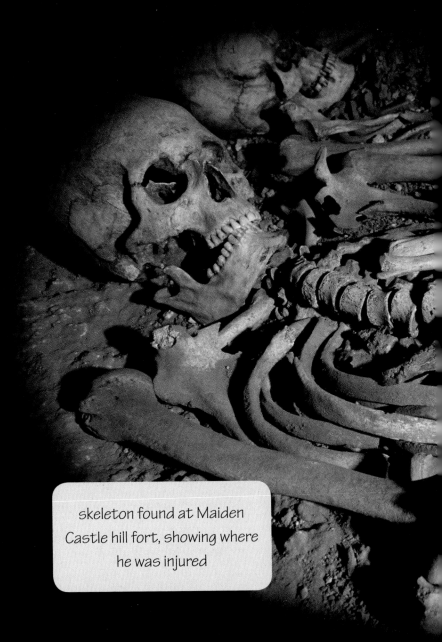

skeleton found at Maiden Castle hill fort, showing where he was injured

ARROWHEAD

In other hill forts, experts have worked out that the gateways may have been burnt down in an attack.

In 43 CE, the Romans invaded Britain. Some hill forts were made stronger at this time, possibly as a defence against the Roman army. Many were abandoned later.

Hill Fort Fact

Over 100 skeletons were found at one hill fort, so there may have been a battle there.

A place to live

Hill forts were safe places in dangerous times, but Iron Age people also used them for other things.

Living

Some hill forts had round houses inside, which shows that Iron Age people may have stayed there. However, it would have been difficult to live inside some hill forts permanently, because there was no water.

Cattle

Iron Age people may have kept their cattle in hill forts, but like people, they couldn't be kept there for a long time without water.

Storing food

In some hill forts, experts have found evidence of buildings that were too small to be houses. Perhaps they were for storing grain. There are so many of these that it's possible that the crops grown in the fields round the base of the hill were brought into the hill fort for safekeeping.

Grain could also be stored in pits dug into the ground, as long as the pit was sealed tightly by putting a layer of clay over the top. The clay kept the air out of the pit and the grain stayed dry. Lots of these pits have been found in hill forts.

A place to meet

Hill forts are easy to see from miles away, so they might have been used in the Iron Age as meeting places for local people. The people gathered there might have discussed important matters and made decisions, or carried out ceremonies and enjoyed feasts.

Hill Fort Fact

Some forts were in use for more than 500 years. That's a lot of feasts!

At one hill fort, more than 140 small pits were discovered. Buried in each pit were items like iron weapons, knives or razors, loom weights, bronze coins, bird bones, sheep skulls and even human bones. These weren't rubbish pits. They show that hill forts may have been special or sacred places, where people met and offered objects to the gods.

A cross-section showing what a pit with offerings would have looked like.

Iron Age treasure

Experts know that Iron Age people had gold jewellery and ornaments like this torc, which was worn around the neck.

Archaeologists have excavated a few of the hill forts in Britain but they haven't found any jewellery like this – yet.

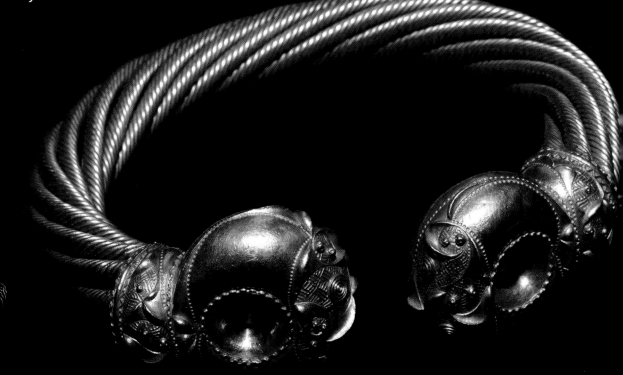

Everyday objects Iron Age people would have used have also been discovered, such as large stones for grinding grain to make flour for bread. In the Iron Age, these items were more important than gold. Cloth kept people warm, and food kept them alive.

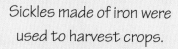

Sickles made of iron were used to harvest crops.

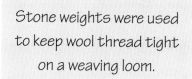

Stone weights were used to keep wool thread tight on a weaving loom.

broken pieces of cooking and storage pots

What happened to hill forts?

Many of the hill forts were not used by Iron Age people after 100 BCE, but others did use the forts.

Roman times

After the Romans invaded Britain in 43 CE, they built temples in some of the empty hill forts. They may have built temples on hills because it made them look more impressive. The Romans used the temples to make sacrifices and offerings to the gods.

Medieval times

Hundreds of years later, at the end of the 11th century, a castle and a cathedral were built inside one fort. There was no need to build new defences as the buildings were surrounded by the mounds of earth made in the Iron Age.

The iron age hill fort at Old Sarum in Wiltshire dates back to around 400 BCE. It was later occupied by the Romans.

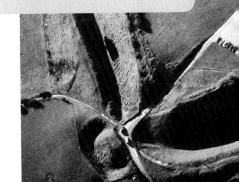

cathedral remains

castle

World War II

More recently, hill forts were used to defend Britain. In the 1940s, during World War II, some hill forts were used as anti-aircraft batteries. Guns were positioned inside and used to fire at enemy aircraft. One hill fort was used as the site of a radar station, protected by dug outs and machine gun posts.

An anti-aircraft battery in action during World War II.

New discoveries

Today, archaeologists are using new technology to discover what lies beneath the earth in some hill forts.

One way they can do this is by using special equipment to fire radar and electrical current into the ground. The radar and electrical current bounce off the stone under the ground and send back a picture to the archaeologists. Experts don't even have to dig up the ground to see what's there, and this means that information can be gathered without disturbing any of the ancient buildings.

scientists using new radar equipment

In 2014, experts studying the hill fort at Old Sarum discovered the remains of a medieval city which had been buried for more than 700 years. This is what experts think Old Sarum may have looked like.

23

A bird's-eye view

So what's left of Iron Age hill forts that you can see without digging or using special machines?

If you look at a hill fort from an aeroplane, what you'll see is ditches and mounds of earth, called "earthworks". After 2,000 years, the wood used to make the ramparts and gates has rotted away, but the earthworks show where the fort once stood.

Hill Fort Fact

One of the smallest hill forts in Britain is the size of nearly four football pitches. One of the largest is the size of 50 football pitches!

Here are the ramparts.

The advantage of looking at hill forts from above is that experts can sometimes see shapes in the ground that might show where a building stood. These shapes and patterns may not be obvious from the ground. Experts also take photographs to record their size and shape. If you walk around a hill fort you'll only be able to see mounds of earth – an aerial photograph shows the whole fort.

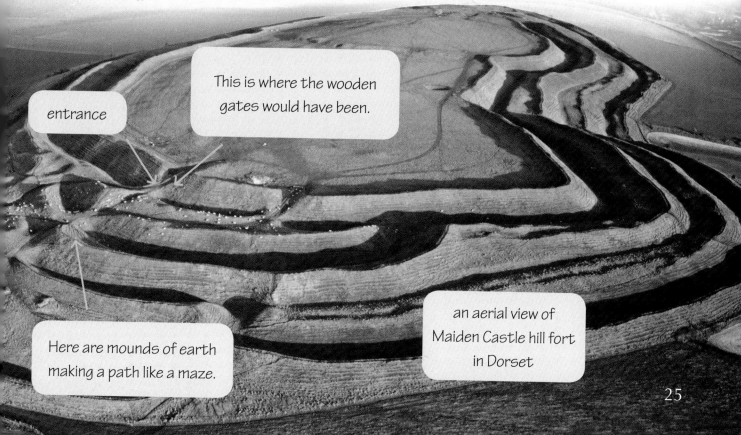

entrance

This is where the wooden gates would have been.

Here are mounds of earth making a path like a maze.

an aerial view of Maiden Castle hill fort in Dorset

It's too late to investigate some hill forts. Half of this fort has fallen into the sea, taking with it some Iron Age secrets. But for the rest of the Iron Age hill forts that can still be seen today, there's more to be discovered under the ground.

Even though Iron Age people couldn't read or write, the objects found inside and around the hill forts tell the story about how people of the past lived, worked, fought and died – 2,000 years ago.

digging for remains on the site of an Iron Age fort at Burrough Hill in Leicestershire

Hill Fort Fact

More than 3,000 hill forts
have been found in Britain.

Glossary

abandoned left behind forever

ancient very old

anti-aircraft batteries a location where weapons are kept, such as guns, to be used as defences against enemy aircraft

archaeologist someone who digs up and studies objects, such as bones and pots, from the past

bartered swapped goods without using money

elaborate with lots of detail

electrical current flow of electricity

embedded set firmly into something

foundations the structure that holds up a building from underneath

javelin light spear thrown as a weapon

ornament object used as decoration

permanently lasting forever

preserve keep safe from harm

radar station place where equipment is used to track the position of aircraft

sacred connected to religion

sickle tool with a long, sharp, curved blade and a short handle, used to cut crops

Index

The hill fort

A place to live

A safe place

A place to visit

A place to fight battles

A place to meet

A sacred place

Ideas for reading

Written by Clare Dowdall, PhD
Lecturer and Primary Literacy Consultant

Reading objectives:
- read for a range of purposes
- discuss understanding and explain the meaning of words in context
- ask questions to improve understanding
- retrieve and record information from non-fiction

Spoken language objectives:
- use spoken language to develop understanding through speculating, hypothesizing, imagining and exploring ideas

Curriculum links: History – the Iron Age; Geography – maps and fieldwork

Resources: materials for model making; whiteboards for fact collection, ICT, paper for drawing.

Build a context for reading

- Ask children to look at the front cover and describe what they can see in the illustration
- Read the blurb with the group. Discuss what hill forts were and ask children to suggest what they might have been used for. Create a context for reading by relating the Iron Age to other eras, stories or events known by the children.
- Look at the word "constructed". Ask children what it means. Can they suggest other words with the same root e.g. "construct-ion", "de-construct", "re-construct". Discuss how we can work out meanings if we understand the root word.

Understand and apply reading strategies

- Ask children to look at the front cover and describe what they can see in the illustration.
- Read the blurb with the group. Discuss what hill forts were and ask children to suggest what they might have been used for. Create a context for reading by relating the Iron Age to other eras, stories or events known by the children.